MW00943694

Songs

to

My

Savior

Volume I

Songs

to

My

Savior

Volume I

Psalms and
Especially for Christmas

Poetry by
Joyce E. Larsen

Copyright © 2013 by
Creations by J.E.Larsen

All rights reserved. Reproduction in whole or any
parts thereof in any form or by any media without
written permission is prohibited.

Second Edition © 2019

Cover Photo by iStockPhoto

This book is dedicated to:
My wonderful Father and Mother –
Lars Rudolph Larsen
Norma Leola Clark Larsen
who taught me to love the Lord, by example.

AND TO:
My dear friend, Larry White –
who listens to Heavenly Father better than I do.

A special thanks to the following people who shared personal stories with me and allowed me to share them with you.

Patrice Baumgardner,
Shellie Malmgren,
Janet Thompson

TABLE OF CONTENTS

PART 1: Psalms

Part 1

Psalms

Songs to My Savior

How shall I ever hallow Him,
my Savior and my King.
Thankful for His mercy –
my soul, before Him, sings.

He knelt there in the garden
and bled from every pore.
And then, He died upon the cross
to save me ever more.

My gratitude is melody,
my faith in Him – the words.
I shall sing with all my heart
until the earth has heard.

My songs unto my Savior,
I sing with love abound;
for Him who suffered selflessly –
true harmony in sound.

Talents

Poetry is a talent,
words perfectly set in place.
The rhyming not so imperative
and could be off a space.

The artist's hand and vision,
the colors brushed onto mat
in such a way, the viewing
shows distance of that which is flat.

The doctor's skill and stoic hand
and ability to learn,
to know to fix the injured flesh,
and alleviate patient's concern.

Every talent shown by man
diminished by all or in part,
when we shall show compassion –
the talent of the heart.

The One

The shepherd has one hundred sheep,
each worthy of watchful care,
grazing in the pasture,
sweet grass for all to share.

And as he gathers all within
the fold – so safe at night.
Ninety and nine are counted for,
one's wandered out of sight.

Good shepherd leaves the ninety nine
still safe within the fold,
out to find the one lost lamb,
to rescue from the cold.

Those left behind do wonder why-
the importance of one so lost,
happy to see the shepherd return
with one, not to know the cost.

Asleep within the shepherd's arms;
don't you know just who I am?
And the cost it took, the shepherd's toll,
saves me – that one lost lamb.

Luke 15: 4 - 7

Music

It's easy for the heart to understand;
when you give a lot through caring,
then the music starts.
For love is the music of the hearts.

Never Give Up

When the temptation seems too much to bear,
and the sprite on your shoulder says no one will care.
May the light in your heart; lit by Father above,
help you never give up – your strength is His love.

Precious Things

Gold and diamonds, rubies and pearls,
are precious things within this world.
To some, a grand car or house to behold,
are precious things, truth to be told.
But while on this earth, praises to sing;
testimony of Christ, my most precious thing.

Believe

I've known the truth of miracles;
that God is in our lives;
when revelation's personal,
affecting closer ties.

I've known the prayer of answers;
of special missions here;
of following a prompting,
the way is very clear.

I've known the gift of knowledge;
believe what some will not;
accepting possibilities –
when help from God is sought.

I've known the burning in the soul
when truth has been received;
a constant prayer within my heart –
truth, only, be believed.

I've known the grace of God who lives,
who hears and answers prayers.
May all who read this, come to know –
He knows and truly cares.

Gethsemane

As a believer in the Christ,
knowing He suffered and prayed;
we might feel He has ransomed us.
Our souls, from sin, He saved.

As we travel along life's path
and we think that we are free;
deep in our hearts, each of us,
faces our own Gethsemane.

Love

We all want love; to find someone
that's wonderful through and through.
When you are giving your love away,
give it to one who deserves it – that's you.

Humility

To kneel, head bowed, before Him.
Accept answer to my prayer
from one so holy given
my soul for to prepare.

To know just how unlearned,
though college degree in my hand.
To stay sincere and teachable
to show just where I stand.

To contritely ask forgiveness,
to repair the pain caused sway,
accepting Christ's pure sacrifice
each and every day.

To follow Him and live His way,
let Him teach me how to be.
It's all in how I look at life
with God given humility.

No Talents?

I have no talents.
No velvet voice,
nor creative hands
that paint and
sketch divine.
A pianist – no.
I never learned,
nor guitar, nor violin.
I cannot knit,
crochet or darn;
or even needlepoint.

"I have no talents."
so you say – like me.
Well –
Have you ever knelt
down to pray,
to glorify your God?
Or smiled at someone
you didn't know?
Or helped someone
who was in need?
Or wept when fire
destroyed a home?

If so, my friend,
you indeed are blessed.
for these also –
are talents.
Some of the greatest
given to man.

Humility and happiness,
love and the ability
to feel other's pain.

I do have talents;
not of the world,
but of God.
I am truly blessed.

Mother

She made our home a heaven,
complete with moon and stars,
and gave each child so much love;
no home, more happy than ours.

She started before we were "thought of"
learning with all her might,
that she would be instrumental
in showing the gospel's light.

One by one, our family grew;
each to learn from the start
how much love our mother had –
for each of us in her heart.

She taught us about the Father
and why He sent us here;
that we might return to heaven
and live in His presence there.

As we grew tall, she was patient
and watched as a shepherd would sheep;
for she knew as Christ once taught,
the seeds that we sow, we reap.

She watched, and taught, and was prayerful
that we would choose to be
loving servants of the Lord
with a place in eternity.

Her light still shines and love's still strong
since we've been out on own.
How grateful we are that she believed
her place was within our home.

Garden

I picture Him in the garden,
alone as He knelt in prayer.
Three times He checked His disciples,
and found them sleeping there.

"Please watch with me." He did entreat,
"That ye enter not into sin."
Withdrawing from them, again He knelt –
and suffered that we might win.

"Father, from me remove this cup."
He prayed to Father above.
"Yet if thou wilt, I'll drink it up."
He did it out of love.

I picture Him in the garden,
the garden Gethsemane.
The agony He suffered –
He suffered it for me.

Matt 26: 38, 42
Mark 14:41
Luke 22: 42 – 44

Eye of the Needle

There stands a long tradition
since ancient days of yore.
Dwellings had a small side gate,
an entrance to the court.

The gate was called a needle;
the doorway was its eye.
Late at night, this gate was used
to enter passersby.

The door, they say, was tiny;
humility, the key.
To make it through the passage,
camels must get on their knees.

Matt 19: 24
Mark 10: 25
Luke 18: 25

Comprehend

I held my puppy in my arms, the day we brought him home.
Tail wagging, happy puppy – I'm not so all alone.
I whispered, as he licked me; a friend, he'd be so true.
"You could never comprehend – how much that I love
you."

I held my sweetheart in my arms on our wedding day.
"Don't they look so charming." Everyone would say.
I whispered, as I cuddled in, when the day was through,
"You could never comprehend – how much that I love
you."

I held my newborn in my arms, the day she came to earth,
knowing I would cherish – her everything from birth.
I whispered, as I watched her and heard her every "coo",
"You could never comprehend – how much that I love
you."

My Father held me in His arms, in heaven, 'fore I left.
Sometimes when life's unbearable, my heart gets so bereft.
He whispers – oh – so softly, when my soul is blue.
"You could never comprehend – just how much – that I
love you."

Become Like Christ

When I serve my neighbor,
and I'm patient with fellow men,
and I easily forgive another,
I start to become like Him.

Memories

Memories come softly,
reminding me of home;
of a loving Heavenly Father
who is there when I'm all alone.
Those memories that whisper
though my heart is in despair.
"There is a purpose for this life."
He'll come if sought in prayer;
if I need Him, He'll be there.

Mission

"My child," My Father told me.
"Life is hard, I'm sure you know.
But remember your special mission –
now it's time for you to go."

The years have flown since that goodbye,
yet there's something in my heart
that tells me I made a promise
to my Father from the start.

When I start to think that life is hard;
I'm not sure I'll make it through.
It's then I remember the promise
to do what He wants me to do.

Each time I am obedient
to His will – in this world of strife,
I know I'm fulfilling a promise
that affects someone else's life.

For I promised to be an example;
serve others with all my might.
That they may know the special love
within the gospel light.

And when I return to my Father
with love so strong in my soul,
for others I've met on this mission,
I'll know that I've met my goal.

Light

My dearest loving Father;
I want Thee proud of me.
Help me to obey Thy will,
so I may return to Thee.

I hope someday that I might be,
a light as Thou are mine;
with love abound in my heart,
so bright that it will shine.

Search the Scriptures

When I read the scriptures,
history begins to unfold.
I see the spiritual side of life,
and God's hand in preserving untold.

And as I've searched the pages,
learned Christ's word and sacrifice then,
I've come to love the scriptures,
for they testify of Him.

John 5: 39

Lullaby

Lullaby, lullaby, my darling.
Lullaby, lullaby, my love.
Lullaby, lullaby, you're a child of God.
So sweet dreams, lullaby, lullaby.

I will sing, I will sing you a lullaby,
as I hold you close in my arms.
Do you know, do you know that God is near?
And He wants you to be happy, lullaby.

You have come from heaven, my little one.
How strong and stalwart you are.
You were born, you were born in these latter-days.
May you feel and heed the spirit, lullaby.

As you grow, as you grow my precious;
may the Lord take you by the hand.
Follow Him, follow Him; He'll show you the way,
and you'll return home to Father, lullaby.

Blessings

Who would have thought an accident
held a blessing in disguise?
For as I sat there shaking,
feeling my demise.

The memory is further now
and no one's badly hurt.
I'm grateful God was with me,
that I was so alert.

Besides a totaled vehicle,
all lives were spared that day,
and insurance paid upon the car –
helped a major debt repay.

So when you see a trial,
look close until you see
what little blessing lurks inside
from God's sense of reality.

... Least of These ...

I stood before a painting
of Christ upon the cross.
Suddenly I knew I felt,
pain at such a loss.

I realized then what I had done
with life before this day.
I knelt before my Savior
and bowed my head to pray.

"Please bless me Lord that I might change,
be someone Thou could use.
Let me be a servant,
to serve as Thou wilt choose."

After I left the building
where the painting hung.
I passed a man who was in need,
yet something held my tongue.

Many times along the way
before I reached my yard;
many people asked for help,
each time my heart was hard.

A blind man, an orphan, a widow;
each needing a helping hand.
Each time I passed without a word,
a kindly deed, command.

That night I knelt beside my bed,
a prayer within my heart.
I said "Dear Lord, please bless me,
that I might know my part."

Looking over the day I spent,
the Lord gave me the key,
'When ye do it to the least of these,
ye have done it unto me.'

Matt 25: 40

Take a Stand

He only was a prophet,
a preacher of holy word,
never born as Son of God,
throughout the world is heard.

So, here, I stand for Jesus Christ.
I know He was so much more,
I know He died for all mankind.
This knowledge is deep to my core.

He is the Savior of the world,
He has taken me by the hand.
I want to live to witness of Him
and I willing take a stand.

Judgment Day

When I am called before the throne,
I'll reap the harvest of seeds I've sewn.
May I have lived in such a way,
that I'll be crowned on judgment day.

Light of Christ

With the wickedness within the world
and the wickedness of men;
it feels all innocence is lost
and Satan's going to win.

It is not easy to do what's right
in a world where right is "wrong",
but remember your goal is beyond this life.
Heaven is where you came from.

You are not here to please someone else,
your stay here is not that long.
Let the light of Christ within your heart
help you to be strong.

Perfection Connection

Jesus Christ was perfect
while he lived on earth.
Everything He said and did
was perfect from His birth.

He truly was the only one
in life to be perfection.
To follow Him will lead me to
my own perfection connection.

Touched

Butterfly kisses,
wispy things;
eyelashes like
butterfly wings.

Lips to pucker,
soft and tender;
forehead soothing,
either gender.

Fingers glide,
soft to fur.
Gentle care,
leads to "purr."

Heart a burning,
truth to find;
soul is soaring.
peace of mind.

Nothing greater,
nothing near it;
being touched
by the Spirit.

Faith

She reached out and touched Christ's cloak,
her faith in Him unwavering.
Her illness instantly revoked;
His countenance unfavoring.

Mark 5: 25 – 34
Luke 8: 43 – 48

The Flame

A flame, a glimmer, a light of Christ;
each soul has at least a spark.
But be sure the flame was lit
by the love in the Father's heart.

Redeemer

He is my God; He is my king.
His praises ever will I sing.
He came to earth to save my soul.
Because of Him, I'll reach my goal.

My Psalm Unto The Father

To praise Thee, God; Thou art my King,
my psalm to Thee, most high,
my heart has yearned to vocalize
throughout the earth and sky.

As pen to paper, flows my love
and gratitude so strong.
To know that I might go someday
somewhere for which I long.

And in the phrasing of my words,
my tears, the ink, become;
that in my psalm to Thee, my God,
my soul's before Thy throne.

Who am I?

Who am I; that He would suffer for me?
This lowly person who has so many
human frailties;
a sinner against Him in so many ways.

Who am I; that He would give up a possible
successful life of riches and fame
to teach and serve others;
only to be killed for it?

Who am I; that He would say
"Come, follow me, and be saved in
eternity, for I have paid the price
of your salvation."

Who am I; a child of God.
I knew and loved Him before the world was.
We knew it was the only way
I might return to God.

Who am I?
Someone who loves Him
as much as He loved me.

A World Without You

When it feels your life is horrible;
you wish you'd not been born.
Take a look at what you've done,
and start to toot your horn.

There's not a person on this earth
who hasn't brought some cheer
somewhere, into someone's life –
far from home, or near.

Can you see your parents solemn;
no new life to hold,
no joy gazing up at them,
no future to behold.

And what about a childhood friend
whose toys you used to share.
See the sadness in her eyes,
oh, so lonely there.

Remember still, that high school boy
you flirted with in class.
No one else would be the same,
to help him – time to pass.

And then, there was a sweetheart
who made your heart strings zing.
There could never be another
who would make his heart so sing.

And walking down some unknown street,
the day you shared a smile
with anyone, it mattered not;
made someone's day worthwhile.

Each time that you were courteous,
each time you said "Hello",
each time you noticed someone else –
helped someone else to grow.

Every person born on earth
brings gladness when they come.
Sometimes, though, they cannot see
their life affected some.

So when your life is horrible,
may God's love help you see –
if truly, you had not been born,
how sad the world would be.

Jesus Wept

What was the cause, the Savior to weep,
His perfection, the body had lain.
For, as He knew, His dear friend was safe,
still He felt the loved ones' pain.

And so we read the scriptures to know,
to sense in His heart, where he kept —
the knowledge of all the loss and the grief.
Mary, Martha — was why "Jesus wept."

John 11: 1 — 44

Ask

Ask and it will be given.
Ask and surely you'll know.
In humble and contrite spirit,
new things to your testament grow.

I've known the answers to asking —
know my Savior has given to me,
not only a way to forgiveness,
but a way to eternity.

Matt 7: 7
James 1: 5

My Birth

On the day of my birth, I drew my first breath
and I opened my eyes the first time.
A new world of hope and minions to try,
a life to be spent – oh, sublime.

On the day of my birth, I'll draw my last breath,
say goodbye to this world that I knew.
I'll open the door to my memories lost,
on to heaven and family so true.

I Know

I know that Jesus died for me.
I know that He paid the cost.
I know my sins – forgiven.
I know I'm no longer lost.

I know there's life everlasting.
I know that my gratitudes show.
I know Christ is my Redeemer.
Least of all, I know that I know.

Carpenter

It's right, He should be a carpenter,
take raw wood – into useful, build.
The same, He takes the untamed soul,
to opportunity, salvation – fulfilled.

I'm Ready

Choose me, dear Savior, I'm ready
to serve and to gratitude give.
To share my faith and knowledge that
I know my Redeemer lives.

Choose me, my Father, I'm ready
to give til my days are done.
To tell the world for every more –
my Savior, is Thine own son.

Choose me, I know I am ready,
in Him, my knowledge is sure.
To live a consecrated life –
my heart will again be pure.

Sabbath

The day is called the Sabbath,
the seventh day of seven.
It's on this day God rested
from creating earth and heaven.

He blessed and sanctified the day.
He blessed and made it holy.
Not just for some to hallow.
but high as well as lowly.

Israel at Sinai
got manna rain at dawn.
The sixth day did they gather
enough for Sabbath morn.

The Sabbath to remember,
commandment, fourth of ten.
A day we rest from labors,
as well as fellow men.

Gen 2: 2, 3
Exodus 16: 4, 5; 15 - 31
Exodus 19: 8 – 11

Answers

All our prayers are answered,
though we sometimes don't believe.
We'd rather feel He didn't hear,
than think He didn't heed.

It is said "God knows our needs"
and wants us to have joy.
But certain things we don't receive;
our faith, we would employ.

When we pray for something
and feel He never heard;
it could be what we prayed for,
but He listened - every word.

When we feel He's silent
and we are feeling low;
it's not He didn't answer,
He just had answered "No".

Recognize

Here on this mortal plain,
it's easy to forget
where I came from –
an ever existing heaven;
and why I am here.

If I should sin
against God's laws,
what chance do I have
to return to His holy presence?

Deep inside my heart,
there is a faintest hope
that grows brighter
when I recognize
the gift given me
two thousand years ago,
in a small garden
and on a lonely hill.

That gift – that changes
everything.
That gift called repentance.

Mortality

I know that I'm only mortal;
have been all of the days of my life.
Held in this frail existence
throughout the pain and the strife.

In the quiet vale of the morning
as I ponder on who I am
and try to make a difference
for those who believe on the Lamb.

These words I write for others,
that help me continue believe,
while I'm still here in mortality –
my Savior to help me retrieve.

The knowledge there's something after;
to live, to love, to see.
Christ's unconditional sacrifice
helps me through mortality.

Reflections

I looked into a mirror
and saw a woman there.
She had a crooked body
with a crooked nose
and crooked teeth.
She was worthless
as the world would see her.

But I took a closer look,
and saw something more
than the world would see.
In the mirror was a woman
with a past unremembered.
A spirit that had been
before the world was.
Who had been valiant
and full of love.
One who was talented
and creative.
A generous spirit who had
strived to build on those talents,
so she might be of greater service
to her fellow man.
There in the mirror,
was a woman so beautiful
that I ached for others to see her.

Will the world ever see
what I see now?
A glorious child of God.

...Are More...

King Ben-hadad of Syria
in Israel did war.
He sought his foes, to ambush them;
his thoughts known by the Lord.

Elisha was the prophet
and warned the Israel king.
Therefore, the king of Syria
was troubled for this thing.

He sent a host and chariots;
encircled Dothan round.
Elisha's servant saw the horde
and told him what he found.

"Alas my master..." he did say.
The man was not alarmed.
Elisha knew, the boy did not.
He knew he'd not be harmed.

"Fear not: for they that be with us
are more than they...with them."
and then he prayed his servant's eyes
be opened and not dimmed.

Opened were the young man's eyes.
He saw a wondrous desire.
For he saw the mountain full
of horses and chariots of fire.

2 Kings 6: 8 - 17

Search

A book of God, a history,
a way of life within,
and as we search the scriptures,
there's a way for us to win.

Blind

When Jesus healed the blind man,
clay, He put upon his eyes.
No sin had caused the blindness,
yet people did him despise.

We go about our business,
through life with no Savior in mind.
And so we overlook holy,
until we are spiritually blind.

John 9: 1 - 41

Converted

Converted am I, in Jesus Christ.
I've taken Him into my heart.
Baptized in His holy name
and so my life – restart.

To follow His precious teachings,
to follow Him to the end,
to be an example of righteousness,
and His gospel – try to defend.

Here spoken, may my humble words,
lead others to know His great love,
to find His loving sacrifice,
to live forward – to see Him above.

Witness

Here is my humble testament
of Him who saves mankind;
the literal son of the living God,
who heaven and earth, did bind.

Born on earth to a virgin
raised by a carpenter's hand.
Unblemished Lamb into the world,
yet no honor within His own land.

I know that Jesus taught virtue,
to retreat from the worldly ways,
to repent of our sins, to follow Him,
to "Samaritan" all of our days.

Greatest of all, this pure knowledge,
so sure, there could never be doubt.
This son of God, my Savior
is what my salvation's about.

For without His loving sacrifice,
to take upon Him, my sin,
I know my eternal soul is lost;
I'd never be able to win.

And so I share this testament
of Him, who gave His life.
My testimony, pure and clear
stands as my witness of Christ.

Peace

There was a man within my life,
so arrogant and mean.
Quite the fool to everyone;
to him, no fault was seen.

He had no compassion;
no pat upon the back.
As I got to know him,
I knew the gifts he'd lack.

I found myself embittered;
things came to him with ease.
But still he had no caring;
his soul was so diseased.

For him, I lost compassion,
I saw within me hate.
All my talents overlooked,
while bosses took his bait.

I joined the crowd that skewered him.
I joined in on the binge.
At just the mention of his name,
my heart within me'd cringe.

One day while I was talking,
I felt so sad inside.
I realized I was losing
the place where peace resides.

I knew why this was happening,
I knew just what to do.
I knew that I was willing,
that I was ready too.

And so, in all humility,
I bowed my head in prayer,
sincerely asking Father –
"Forgive me" – then and there.

I asked that all my anger
toward this man to cease,
and every time I heard his name,
within my heart be peace.

I know my prayer's been answered.
I've gone along my way.
This man has shown no changes –
but I've got peace today.

songstomysavior.com

If you are into poetry
and have a love for God,
then enter in and get your fill.
You, too, can give Him laud.

My heart is full with love and thanks
to Father and His Son.
Because of them, I'll have a chance,
my errors overcome.

And so you see, just why I've done
the praises that I have.
My goal: to share with all the world
His everlasting Salve.

And if you like what you read here -
note poetry in print.
No matter where you are in life,
to touch, as fire's flint.

Forgive Me

My life has not been perfect.
I've sinned, and mistakes are sure.
But I've known the grace of Jesus Christ;
through Him – my soul can be pure.

I don't expect blank forgiveness,
I've chosen my errs to repent,
for I know there's more to life changing,
when accepting Christ's sacrifice spent.

Mansions

My mansion is a cozy shack,
smallish in its size,
with library and living room,
around my soul it lies.

I've heard it said that mansions
set us all apart;
to each – our size of building –
is opposite of heart.

From the Heart

Mere words.
No eloquence of tongue,
or perfectly placed metaphors
can intimidate such devoted passages.
For simple is the heart felt praise
that comes from a child's lips.
And child - like are prayers
that blossom on the tongues of
those who never knew poetry.

Mere words.
Untouched by sculptor's pen,
and uncluttered by thoughtless similes.
For what pen can capture the true
spirit of love felt for the divine?
No manner of poetry penned,
no matter how elite the style,
can touch the true and simple poetry
that comes from a grateful heart.

Hunger

I feel an aching hunger,
like the kind at the end of a fast.
A physical kind when your stomach
tells you food is needed to last.

But this hunger is not about nature.
It's eternal and never to end.
To hunger and thirst after righteousness,
a hunger I always will tend.

Matt 5:6

Tender Heart

It's moved upon by something sad,
sorrow gives when someone's bad.
It's brought to weep upon God's part
when truth is given – tender heart.

Golden Rule

When driving down the highway
or in a grocery line,
talking in a library
or at the "Movies Nine".

All around are people,
be known or stranger there.
All our actions t'ward them
lasting through every care.

If we are considerate,
use the "what would I like" precious tool,
then, I'm sure, it's not just conscience –
we are living the Golden Rule.

Worship

Father in Heaven, I worship Thee
and love Thee to eternity's end.
For in Thy great wisdom saves my soul
and Thy only begotten to send.

Father, Thou knowest that flesh is weak.
No sinner to perfect become
without an unblemished sacrifice,
who'd be Thy begotten son.

Thy only begotten son on earth,
the Messiah, the Holy Lamb.
He suffered for all the sins of the world –
my Savior, the great I AM.

To Jesus Christ, my gratitude fills
the infinite space in my heart.
For, though to try, I'll never repay
what He's given me from the start.

And so my words can never expound
the love deep inside that I feel.
Only to know, if I live the right way,
I'll be with Thee eternally, still.

Daddy

As a child, my hand in yours,
looked up into your eyes.
You picked me up and held me tight,
yet careful for my size.

I was one of many,
I clamored for your touch.
And when you hugged and kissed me,
it meant so very much.

I didn't know, all cuddled in
your massive, careful arms;
I didn't know my time with you,
so short, not without charms.

We managed through those few short years,
not dwelling on the past;
I feel it still – your presence –
and love, a life, to last.

Knock

There is a door upon my soul,
my spirit lives inside.
I'll wait until my Savior comes
and then, with Him, abide.

I shall know when He arrives,
it's what I'm waiting for.
For when He comes to visit,
He'll knock upon my door.

I hear somebody knocking,
I'll open up to Him.
Behold, He's standing at the door
that opens from within.

Rev 3: 20

Feel Thy Love

God, I know I'm imperfect,
but I know that I'm loved by Thee.
And that Thy love's unconditional,
no strings attached to see.

Sometimes, I feel unworthy
as I sit and I contemplate.
I feel so far below the mark,
I feel a world of hate.

Father, I come before Thee,
knowing that it's different above.
Help me reduce these human self doubts –
please help me to <u>feel</u> Thy love.

Endure

When I see a trial in my path,
I know there's a bump in the road.
A dilemma, I have to overcome
to make it to my abode.

Not ever easy to make it past
the mountain, to find the cure,
but courage grows, continue on –
by each trial that I endure.

My Destiny

I was not born here on earth to fail,
I'm a winner through and through.
I need to remember, to trust God above
to find strength within me a-new.

The road I have chosen here on earth
is not easy, but that is the key.
I'm here to serve others, to build my own strength,
for heaven's my destiny.

Whole

Better today than yesterday,
each day I strive to be.
Look forward to tomorrow
and on into eternity.

It's not meet that I be perfect
today nor yet this eve.
Just need to change one certain thing,
one thing, I can achieve.

Morrow after morrow
finds me changing toward my goal,
so when I reach here – after,
I'll be completely whole.

Hold On

When trouble is all around you
and you're unable to pay its price,
look forward unto His forgiveness –
hold onto the hope of Christ.

Innocent

Innocent is the baby,
just come from heaven above.
New to life possibilities,
and share in her parent's love.

Innocent is the victim
of crime so violently done.
But with the hope of recovery
and a chance to overcome.

Only one – to live on earth,
free of negativity spent.
Only one, our Savior, tis true,
of wrong-doing is innocent.

Hearken

Let me hearken unto Thy truths
spoken of by Thy prophets on earth.
Let me hearken unto Thy will,
a desire, almost, since birth.

Let me hearken unto Thy words,
recorded so we could receive;
words Thou hast spoken – almost to hear –
Thy voice, until we believe.

Let me hearken unto Thy heart
that loves more than we can know,
and may I live to shine Thy light –
that surely my harkening will show.

My Friend

You made my life worthwhile.
You gave me – purpose back,
because you trusted Father
and faith you didn't lack.

You showed me that believing
is knowing heaven's voice.
You taught me that the spirit
can come through one so choice.

Thank you for encouragement
to help me trust His will
and follow His desire of me;
the feeling's with me still.

My heart is full of gratitude;
our friendship, only brief.
But still, I owe you everything
and wish your soul relief.

My friend, I want to thank you.
I needed, you were there.
When you followed Father's prompting,
you were the answer to my prayer.

Come Home

It doesn't matter what you've done,
God loves you anyway.
His love has no conditions
on what you do or say.

Although His love's eternal
and always stays the same,
a broken law has consequence
and always places blame.

Your Father up in heaven
knew this to be true,
and so He planned a Savior
who'd take the blame for you.

Father's only goal for earth
was have His children win.
The only way we sinners could –
was someone ransom sin.

So our loving brother
took all the pain to bear,
that we might use the ransom;
return to Father there.

Dear child of the living God,
great blessings are foretold.
Please use the gift Christ gave to us;
come back into the fold.

Refiner's Fire

I've heard the story – refiner's fire,
the worker of silver and gold.
How did he know when the piece was complete,
as it sat there, before it was cold.

The refiner had said through heat and through stress,
as he worked with the metal in place;
he knew it was done when he brought it up close
and in mirror, he'd see his own face.

And so I know, it's that way with me –
I am silver, refiner is God.
I'll be complete through refiner's fire,
His reflection, of where I have trod.

God's Word

In all of the world
there's no perfect man –
but the truth of God's words
always will stand.

Pick Me Up

The Christus stood before us,
majestic on its stand,
surrounded by the universe;
with loving outstretched hands.

I felt such love within me,
I felt the spirit strong.
Seeing Christ's similitude
made me think of home.

With us, my small daughter,
eyes lofted to its face.
She studied so intently
each feature carved with grace.

I watched her gaze into his eyes.
What wonder did she see
that kept her young attention.
Whatever could it be?

My question, then was answered.
The answer, quite abrupt.
She raised her arms toward him
so he could pick her up.

Watching

On a cold and rainy day
I went about my work,
unaware that someone's eyes
watched me like a hawk.

I felt it and I turned around,
but no one else was there.
Who could spy and not be seen;
who, alone, would care?

That night, as I was dreaming,
I saw just who it'd be.
For all day long, every day,
God watches over me.

Ten Virgins

Ten of us to meet the groom,
coming tonight it is said.
Each with a lamp and oil;
each lamp lit in its stead.

Half of us were wise enough
to have extra oil near;
for none of us know the hour
the bridegroom will appear.

The hour grows late; wicks grow dim;
each lamp's oil is slight.
Still the groom has not arrived;
the call comes, he is nigh.

"Share of thy oil", five entreat.
"Lest we have no fuel for flame."
The five who were wise answer; "No,
lest our own lamps shall do the same."

"Go ye out to the venders
and buy some oil there:
we brought enough for our own lamps,
we haven't enough to spare."

While they are out buying oil,
the bridegroom does arrive.
The virgins, wise, enter in,
but not the other five.

The wedding begins behind locked doors;
five come with oil bought,
saying "Lord, Lord. Open to us."
But he answers "I know you not."

Ten of us to meet the groom.
coming tonight by decree.
Five are foolish, five are wise.
Which of the ten are we?

Matt 25: 1 - 12

Family

I'm part of a great big family;
nine siblings, each a catch.
Each with our own personality,
and love enough to match.

I'm part of a great big family;
greater than seas of sand.
Each to be known by Father above;
it's the family of man.

Accountability

Each decision that I make,
I'm sure affects the whole.
For every choice, whether good or bad
I am accountable.

Our Savior

He died upon a lonely hill;
Calvary was its name.
Third day, the Lord was risen;
the world was not the same.

He suffered in Gethsemane
and bled from every pore.
In doing so, gave us the key
to open salvation's door.

He taught the sermon on the mount;
the masses gathered near.
He showed the path to heaven,
if we, but only hear.

He was born to save the world;
how lowly was His birth.
But on that holy star-lit night
our Savior came to earth.

Relief

When I'm feeling lonely,
or when I'm feeling low.
When I feel imperfect
while those around me glow.

When I feel below the mark
or that I'll never win.
When I count up all my faults,
and each and every sin.

When I wonder why I fail
or why I always lose;
why, it seems, that no one cares
or why I wrongly choose.

Sometimes when I need it most
and pray in pain and grief,
a calmness comes all over me
and brings my soul relief.

To each that feels such sorrow,
no matter when or where,
our Father up in heaven
always will be there.

The Hour

I was there at the hour of His birth,
I sang in the heavenly choir.
To herald His coming "Peace be on Earth".
The earth was no longer in mire.

I was there at the hour of His death,
as He hung upon the cross.
I saw the earth in turmoil,
in reaction to such a loss.

May I be there at the hour of the end,
when He comes a second time.
May I have lived the kind of life –
that, the joy to see Him, is mine.

Love is the Most Powerful Word

Of all the words – lips spoken,
no matter the language heard,
when sharing with another,
"Love" is the most powerful word.

Spiritual Nature

Sunset in the western sky
complete with reds and golds.
A masterpiece of beauty,
just part – that nature holds.

Majestic are the redwoods
or humble local pines;
nature's spirit deep within –
the role that God defines.

Wild flowers in a meadow,
mountain towering above;
all retrospect of virtue
and sharing of God's love.

When we commune with nature,
it's like we take God's hand.
For nature's very reverent –
as the spirit is, of man.

Miracles

The rising sun, the moon, the stars;
the birds flying in the skies;
all of the facets of nature,
all miracles in my eyes.

The human body, arms and legs,
a mind of cognoscente view;
to see and hear, to touch and smell –
all aspects of living, too.

The turning water into wine,
the raising of the dead,
giving sight unto the blind,
and all that Jesus did.

When you look at anything –
no matter big or small,
everything around us
is of God – they're miracles – all.

Heart to Heart

I saw you on a crowded street.
My eyes met yours, but it was brief.
I knew, you knew not what to say;
twas in your eyes, we looked away.

Then we passed, as ships at night.
No thought again til out of sight.
Not before and not again
would we meet – til end of men.

Why was I so drawn to you?
Deep inside, I know it's true;
I knew you well – before this part;
that's why we spoke – heart to heart.

May God above guide your way,
comfort give until the day,
when we, dear friend, again will meet
with memory fresh, at Jesus' feet.

Defend or Deny

Sunset over cast shadows.
Alone in my thoughts,
with multitudes around me.
Listening brings salt laden tears.
What blasphemy against my Lord.
Yet something holds my tongue.

"...and Peter remembered the word
of Jesus..."

Stars shine, glistening on endless black.
Solitude far from my presence;
a conversation is overheard.
'There is no God in heaven.'
Yet something holds my tongue.

"...before the cock crows, thou shalt deny
me thrice..."

Sun rises above color kissed mountain peaks,
waiting for a signal of dawn.
Quiet is broken by sounds of disbelief.
The gospel, they say, cannot be true.
Yet something holds my tongue.

"...and he went out, and wept bitterly."

Matt 26: 75

"Your Needs Will Be Met"

Sat on the floor, beside my bed,
after kneeling for morning prayers.
A heavy burden on my heart,
and sadness all over – was there.

Tears were streaming from my eyes,
because heart and head both knew,
not only was life falling apart,
but my car was that way too.

And as I cried, a certain peace
came over me, just set.
And in my mind, three times, I heard
a voice – "Your needs will be met."

I dried my eyes and drove to work,
and made it about half way
when my little car "threw a rod"
and I called out for the day.

My brother came and got me;
to sister's house, we went
and talked about my dilemma
when suddenly she said "rent."

She knew someone who'd lease their car
just for a month or three,
and that would help to get me where
a new car could work for me.

Later on my sister asked
why no concern I'd show.
I told her of my morning prayer
and had watched God's answer flow.

Deep inside – my humbled mind
knows the comfort, that morning, I felt
had stayed with me throughout that day,
helped through what adversity dealt.

To Live an Inspired Life

I strive to feel the spirit,
to follow where it leads,
and live by Christ's example
while trying to succeed.

My life is full of ups and downs,
sometimes my "ox is mired".
But surely I will make it through
if I can live a life inspired.

My Truths Received

I know there's a Heavenly Father,
I know I'm a child of God.
I know I've a Savior named Jesus Christ
who suffered for sins I had trod.

I know these things more surely
than the sun in the east does rise.
For the Holy Spirit has touched my heart,
left no question in my eyes.

Include Me

Include me when you're doing a birthday card
or a present for someone at work.
For, oh, how I love to share these things
and responsible never to shirk.

Include me when you're counting your circle of friends
you can call on when you are blue.
You know you mean the world to me
and there's nothing I wouldn't do.

Include me when you're asking God for grace
for those who've committed sin.
For although I'm living a Christian life,
I know what my actions have been.

But, most of all, when you're counting those
who'd sing praises from mountain to sea –
for gratitude given – Christ's sacrifice,
remember, please, include me.

My Prayer

I wish I knew just how to pray,
and how to speak my heart,
and how to get an answer
I'm sure is from my God.

I know he hears and answers prayers.
I'm sure He has – my own.
I know He watches over me
when I am all alone.

Then why, when troubled is my soul,
I feel so far away,
and feel my prayer's not answered
or "wrong" – as they would say.

I long to know His will of me
when kneeled in humble prayer.
Yet, still, there is no answer
even though I feel Him there.

This prayer, I pray in earnestness,
although my heart is still;
I pray that God will guide my way
that I might do His will.

Looketh on the Heart

When Samuel, the prophet, to Bethlehem was sent,
to find, anoint another who'd rule where God had lent.

When he saw Eliab, thought he'd be the chosen king.
God gently spoke into his mind, rebuked him for this
thing.

"Look not upon the outside – for chosen is he not.
Men look upon appearance, God looketh on the heart".

As we live upon the earth, should take this thought to
kind.
for genes determine beauty, but heart determines mind.

1Samual 16: 7

A Smile

As I go about my daily life,
God's prompted me to smile
at people all around me;
their sorrows fade a while.

I know my life's not perfect,
Yet, still, the prompting's there;
to smile at another
and love for people, share.

I am very grateful –
the promptings that I've heeded;
a smile's always welcome
and sometimes, it is needed.

A Brand New Life

It begins with taking one short breath
when out of the water you come.
You feel a new life given to you
and a sense that now you belong.

Each new step and forward go,
like a baby learning to walk.
New things to know, forgiveness earned,
a whole new world to unlock.

Take Christ by the hand, follow His way;
commandments, beatitudes keep.
And as you move on, the spirit you'll know –
testimony to get and grow deep.

Surely you'll know the depth of His love,
and to know you'll be saved by grace.
Give thanks to our God, again you were born,
and someday a heaven to face.

Sisters

There's a photo on the mantel.
Three sisters sitting close.
In hats, they look so charming,
and smiling; so composed.

Sitting on a porch step,
no shoes upon their feet;
such love is seen between them,
sisterhood complete.

Three sisters who'd known happiness;
three sisters who'd known grief;
now separate by distance,
but there – to share relief.

The photo of the sisters
alone, the only one,
sits upon the mantel
where memories belong.

When I see the photo,
all cares within me flee.
I love my sisters dearly;
I'm glad I'm one of three.

Beyond the door

In every life, there is a door,
a door we'll all go through –
that leads from here to after,
from life to something new.

When the door is opened,
most welcome other side,
within a new existence,
a place where peace resides.

The loved ones who are left behind
hold sorrow in the heart.
May God of all creation
make painful feelings short.

For love that's felt for those on earth,
unchanged for evermore;
still there, when reunited,
when we go beyond the door.

Rainbows

God has not promised sun always to shine,
soft fragrant flowers, our pathway, to line.
Nor has He promised us skies always blue
or people around us to trust, who'll be true.
But in all our living, the highs and our lows,
when, sometimes it showers, God give us rainbows.

…Be Much Required

A believer in Christ, you are on your way,
your knowledge and talents inspired.
Remember, when counting His gifts to you,
"…much is given… shall be much required".

Luke 12: 48

Beauty

When Isaiah prophesied that Christ
would come to save mankind,
he spoke of things to look for,
all prophesy to bind.

One thing Isaiah told the world
that we should take undimmed.
"he hath no form or comeliness…
that we…desire Him."

It's beauty, throughout history
desired of man from birth.
Remember, though, uncomely
was the Savior of the earth.

Isaiah 53: 2

Baa

Grazing in the meadow,
safe under shepherd's care.
When evil starts to lurk around,
the shepherd's staff is there.

Like all the sheep, I know His voice
and He knows who I am.
When he calls for me to come –
I'll surely follow Him.

John 10: 27

The Widow's mites

Christ taught in the temple –
the last week of His life,
and sitting near the treasury,
saw a widow throw two mites.

He said to His disciples
that what she gave that day
was more than anybody else –
for, of her want did pay.

As others gave unto the fund,
abundance, did they have.
But when the widow tossed those mites,
twas everything she gave.

So if you see around you,
one, give little to the toll.
In abundance seems like nothing,
but they may have given all.

Mark 12: 42

Warfare

There is a battle in my soul,
waging since my birth.
Good and evil fighting there –
the purpose for this earth.

As I fight this battle,
it's all in how I choose.
In my weakness, God gives strength;
for I can't afford to lose.

Every moment, every day,
my good side battles sin.
If needed, God sends extra help.
It's a battle I can win.

Savior

I know that Jesus died for me;
He suffered and prayed in Gethsemane.
He asked that "Father remove this cup."
Then, in agony, sweat drops of blood.

He offered himself as a sacrifice;
and for me, He willing paid the price.
If I would repent and humbly accept
the ransom He lovingly paid for my debt.

I know I'm imperfect while on this earth.
I made some poor choices after my birth.
My choices have left on my soul, a great stain.
Without Him, I'll not see my Father again.

If I will employ the gift that He gave
and try to be like Him, my soul He will save.
When life is over; my Savior I'll greet,
with grateful tears, I'll shower His feet.

Luke 22: 42 - 44

"...More to Life..."

There was a time within my life,
deep sadness covered me.
Depression is the word we use,
in world to this degree.

I don't believe to take one's life
is answer ever called.
Yet in this state of massive pain,
is how my pain resolved.

I sat, and cried, and prayed to God –
this thing I ached to do.
"Oh, please, my Father, help me –
my plan, I don't ensue."

And as I cried, a phone call,
the answer to my prayer.
Upon the line, the other end –
a friend from work was there.

She asked me to a movie.
She'd pick me up in "ten".
I knew she was the answer
I'd prayed for – even then.

But still more help was waiting,
the thing to change my life.
A small line from the movie,
deep soul, as would a knife.

And when the movie ended,
we talked about the way
she wondered of her prompting –
why me upon this day.

I told her of my sadness,
She smiled, then we cried.
My need and her acceptance
of prompting or I died.

Even, after all these years,
my memory is strong,
and gratitude I'm living,
to her and God belong.

But how I knew her prompting
was answer to my prayer?
Not a phone within her house;
she walked to call me there.

And what about that little line –
script writer, by request.
Years later would retrieve a life –
"There's more to life, than death,
Jim."

From "The Man from Snowy River"

God is Love

As you think about your sweetheart
or your newborn from above,
or those within your family –
remember – God is love.

1 John 4: 7, 8

I Am Here

As life rushed all around me,
new pains drew ever near.
In anguish, loud, I spouted –
"God, do you know that I am here?"

Amidst my lamentations,
God's answer was so clear;
softly came into my mind –
"Do you know that I am here."

Dearly

There is one whom I love dearly,
and my love moves me longer;
when my knowledge of what He did for me
makes my gratitude grow stronger.

Joy in Heaven

Every person born on earth
has committed some err, that's true.
Yes, everyone a sinner,
everyone including you.

Christ taught us that repentance
the sinner can employ.
For every sinner that repents,
in heaven, there is joy.

Luke 15: 7, 10

"Thou Hast Said"

I see them in the upper room,
Passover meal was set.
Christ said one should betray Him,
disciples wondered, met.

To each who asked "Is it I?"
His answer – not to dread.
Then Judas asked him "Is it I?"
Christ answered "Thou hast said".

When, we in life, our actions be,
as asking, we betray?
May our dear Lord, the Son of God
ever answer "Nay".

Matt 26: 21 – 25

Just Who Do You Think You Are?

At three years old, I flour the house,
I run, but don't get too far.
Grabbed up to face that angry voice,
"Just who do you think you are?"

Near seventeen, at home alone,
without asking, I take the car.
When I get home, my father yells,
"Just who do you think you are?"

When twenty nine, out on a date,
the guy wants to lower the bar.
When I say no, his anger flairs,
"Just who do you think you are?"

Now middle aged at fifty four,
life changed, cause of Bethlehem's star.
And as I give praise, I hear curt calls,
"Just who do you think you are?"

Golden years set, no mind my age,
I've worked hard for the holy Lamb.
As I close my eyes unto God's rest –
I know exactly who I am.

Think

I think of how He suffered,
I think of how He died.
I think of resurrection,
and where His body laid.

I think of all the miracles,
I think of stories heard.
I think of all His actions,
and each and every word.

I think of His example,
I think about His birth.
I'm grateful for my Savior
and why He came to earth.

Entertain

There is a knock upon my door.
Should I let her in.
She is a stranger to my sight,
but looks so very thin.

I open up my home to her.
Share food and clothing clean,
a nice warm bath and bedding soft,
til morning to be seen.

In morning's light, her stomach full,
gave thanks – to leave a new.
When she turns to walk away,
a wing slips into view.

When we help some unknown soul
and think it's so inane,
as now, I know, twas unaware –
it's angels, we entertain.

Hebrews 13: 2

"Let My People Go"

Moses said to Pharaoh,
"My God has sent me so
that I would come and tell you
'Let my people go…'"

Pharaoh's heart was hardened,
not touched by pleas or begs.
The people, he would not set free,
so God sent Egypt plagues.

The rod turned to a serpent,
the Nile became blood;
both frogs and lice tormented,
then flies – they came as flood.

Each time that God told Moses
to ease the people's woe –
go tell the Pharaoh, God has said
"Let my people go…"

But Pharaoh would not listen,
each time he would not yield,
and so the plagues continued,
each worsened as they'd build.

The cattle died, the skies spit hail,
locust, darkness reigned.
But Pharaoh's heart stayed hardened
til death of first born came.

Without request, did Pharaoh cry,
at last he felt the blow.
He now called Moses to him –
and let the people go.

The Israelites left quickly,
no leaven bread did take.
Soon Pharaoh's heart was hardened,
his decision did forsake.

With chariots and horses,
he sought Israel to claim,
to capture and to bring them
back to Egypt once again.

God was to keep his promise,
his people to be free,
and as the Pharaoh followed,
Moses parted the Red Sea.

Israel crossed upon dry land,
once safe on other side,
the Pharaoh's army following,
sea water covered, died.

With Red Sea now between them
and Egyptians drown within,
the Israelites were truly safe;
God's people – to follow Him.

Exodus 5 – 14

Christ's Life

A manger was His cradle;
gold and spices did they bring.
Eight days old when to temple,
then His life sought by a king.

To Egypt where they found safety.
A carpenter, He became.
Then, at the age of thirty,
He began to earn His name.

He was baptized by emersion,
taught the sermon on the mount.
His stories were called parables,
and miracles hold count.

He said He was the son of God,
to fulfill the Mosaic law.
He was the sacrificial Lamb,
in whom there was no flaw.

For all mankind He suffered
in the garden and on the hill.
And then, He was resurrected
in fulfillment of Father's will.

Christ's life was selfless giving,
His path not an easy one.
His final sacrifice was borne
for all, by God's own son.

Matt 2:11, 13; Matt 3:13, 16; Matt 5 – 7; Matt 5:17; Matt 8:2, 29 Matt 13:3, 55 Matt 28: 1 – 6;
Mark 6:3;
Luke 2:12, 21 – 27; Luke 3:23; Luke 22: 41 – 44;
John 12: 47

Unfailing

Elijah sat at Zarephath's gate,
saw a woman gathering wood.
Asked of her, for water
and then, for bread, if could.

Long famine in the country,
barrel only a handful of meal.
The oil cruse near empty –
to last, just once, then nil.

She told the man her story,
last time – her son to eat.
Then they would die together
in this sad tale of defeat.

Elijah gave her a promise,
if make a cake for him first,
the meal and the oil never to fail
til the day that the earth lost its thirst.

She followed the prophet's council
and fed to him last of the bread.
Then, back in the house, she did find
meal and oil, unfailing, in stead.

1 Kings 17: 10 – 16

Other Sheep

Jesus is called the good shepherd;
so He said while He was alive.
He knew His sheep and they knew Him,
heard His voice, followed and thrived.

The Savior said He had other sheep.
Sheep – that were not of that fold,
and those same sheep shall hear His voice.
He would bring and one group behold.

Here is my heart, and my question.
May you hear it and heart it to keep.
Why would the Lord talk about them –
and where would there be other sheep.

John 10:16, 27

Conversion

Someone once asked, "Do you believe in Christ?"
And a flood of thoughts came to mind.
A simple answer could suffice,
but the answer, I wanted to bind.

And so I began "Let me tell you,
just how my belief in Him goes –
that in my sharing, the spirit –
will touch your heart til it shows."

Begin by looking at the world,
so complex and integral move.
There must be a higher power,
a god is in place – such truth.

And so the spiritual side of me grew
to believe that a God watches all,
Began, be aware of my rights and my wrongs –
what then, for surely I'd fall.

To know, became my earnest desire,
set aside the desires of flesh.
To read, to study the scriptures,
to learn God's desires afresh.

That there is a design for living –
each soul to earth did come,
and every one a child of God
to know that we could go "home".

But how to return to heaven
with wrongs so heavy in heart?
Twas a plan put in place by Father
to save us from the start.

A Savior, a pure unblemished lamb
would die and set us free,
would take my sins upon Himself;
such love to that degree.

And as my testimony grew,
each truth sank deep to soul.
I knew and prayed my Savior
would help to reach my goal.

So, do I believe in Jesus Christ?
"He's my Savior, My God." My soul screams.
No greater knowledge of anything
comes to mind or greater means.

Because I know I'm imperfect,
my love and gratitude worth –
that I may help convert others
and sure knowledge to fill the whole earth.

Prayer

When I get down on my knees,
hope starts glistening.
Every time I say a prayer,
I know God's listening.

Happy

I sit here in my sadness,
I think of sadding things.
There's a light off in the distance –
a light that happy brings.

It lightens up my darkness.
My heart, it warms – no cease,
to where my sadness disappears
and in its place is peace.

And peace is such a funny thing,
for when it stays a while,
soon happy comes to join it
and frown replaced by smile.

Father Holds You

Your mother held you in her arms
when hunger first you knew.
And in that moment, you knew not
I, too, was holding you.

And when you rode your bicycle
and fell and skinned your knee,
limping to those comfort arms;
first comfort hold was me.

Your first true love who broke your heart –
the pain you had to bear.
You cried aloud through sobbing tears,
my rocking arms were there.

And when not chosen for the job
that you were perfect for.
The pain you felt within your heart,
I shared, and held you more.

When sorrow was to illness,
the pain you felt was real.
I would never leave your side –
I held you 'til you healed.

The greatest sorrow one can know,
yet time apart is brief.
To lose the one you love so much –
I held you in your grief.

Throughout your life – from birth to end,
whenever pain is near –
my arms will be around you,
know Father holds you dear.

Purposes

Three years ago, I wrote a poem.
Inspired, that, I knew.
I felt that I was writing
God's love for someone blue.

The poem, itself, had touched my soul,
I loved it from the start.
But set aside with other work,
soon memory to part.

This year my job had brought me to
a friend from many years.
And when she saw me coming t'ward -
she burst out – into tears.

We greeted, hugged and said "Hello".
Our happiness we glowed.
But, later on, she mentioned,
a little sadness showed.

I had with me by happenstance,
the book that held that poem.
What miracle was coming
that brought it from my home.

As I read the poems I wrote,
I read this loving end,
and felt the urge come over me –
to share it with my friend.

Next day, I knew I had the chance.
I shyly asked to read.
And as I read, I saw in her
some answer to a need.

I knew the poem had touched her heart
the way it had my own.
I didn't know til later
God's planning – it had shown.

She told me of her turmoil
had set some sadness in,
and that the poem I read to her,
the comfort it had been.

Yet, later, still, I pondered –
what promptings had been spurred.
Then came, in rushing – answers.
That poem, I penned – for her.

And so I share this story –
God's love for each of us.
Poem titled "Father Holds You",
He planned three years to touch.

Angel

Oh, that I were an angel,
to have my heart's desire.
My testimony vocalize,
to touch the heart like fire.

I would call from mountain tops
with words phrased just the way
that all who heard, would know the truth
my heart would have to say.

Oh, that I were an angel,
my yearning, aching plea –
to know the perfect way to touch
your yearning soul – to see.

This sure unshaken knowledge,
I never could deny.
Christ, the Lord, the King of kings
for all my sins, did die.

And for you too, He shed His blood,
took on Himself, your sin.
Should we repent and follow Christ,
we'll live with Him again.

So may desire fill your soul
to know, yourself, His grace.
That in so knowing, in the end –
you'll see His loving face.

Oh, that I were an angel,
my heart's desire fulfill.
To share the love I have for Christ,
grows stronger in me still.

My Testimony

My soul knows and loves Christ.
I know that He lives.
He suffered and died that I might return
to God.
He is my Redeemer and I shall have
eternal life.
Through Him, my sins shall be forgiven.

My heart aches to know that He had to suffer,
and I weep to think I've caused Him pain.
But, as my soul feels sorrow now,
so it will soar to see Him
in the royal courts on high.

I believe in Him with every fiber of
my being.
There is no question that holds back my song.
I shall sing my song of redeeming love
and gratitude until the end of eternity.

I know He descended below all things;
that He will return triumphant to reign on earth.
If I live righteously, I will be caught up
in that great day to meet Him.

This is my testimony of Him who died and
lives again;
clothed in immortality and eternal life.
He has shown me the path that I should trod.
He is my Redeemer, my Lord, my Savior, my King.
In His holy name. Amen

Part 2
Especially for Christmas

Dedicated to:

My dear Savior, Jesus Christ –
the reason for the season

What Christmas Means to Me

What does Christmas mean to me?
Earth's kindnesses increase,
more people give of self and help,
which causes greater peace.

On the lighter side, it's said
that happiness and joy
also grow, good cheer to be
for every "girl" and "boy".

For most, when having family 'round
brings back much childhood cheers.
A time to share what's happening,
catch up with closest "peers".

For me it's time to look at self,
what inventory can.
Decide what changes – try to make,
to better who I am.

Last on this list, but not in life,
look at the reason be.
My Savior's birth – to save my soul,
born holy, error free.

Candy Cane

A shepherd's crook, they call it –
the staff that shepherds use
while watching over sheep at night –
protection, do they choose.

The crook is made of wood cut straight
and curved along the top.
The shepherd's staff, a walking stick,
yet, wolf or danger stop.

Envisioning the shepherd's crook,
know that the shepherd's Christ.
He was born to save mankind,
protect through sacrifice.

And when we see a candy cane,
all wrapped in red and white,
may we see the Shepherd's love –
blood shed and glory light.

Bells

Hush, be quiet, so to hear
the sound so clear and pure.
Can you tell the simple tones
combined for music sure?

For on this night, this holy night
is born, our Christ the king.
And to announce his holy birth –
the bells of heaven ring.

Christmas Tree

Christmas tree, oh Christmas tree,
how green your branches grow,
and in the newness look of spring
renewal life you show.

Candles lit upon your limbs,
and tinsel hangs there too.
The ornaments adorn your look,
a star on top of you.

As we look and draw the warmth,
you share from tip to toe.
May we remember, that you mean –
Christ's coming, also glow.

Ornament

The ornaments upon the tree
collected through the years,
each chosen for its meaning,
remembrance, appears.

Each set precisely in its place,
attached with loving care.
The memories of Christmas past,
each ornament does share.

The ornaments I've hung this year
have touched me, every one.
From sleighs to Santa, antique to glass,
handmade to stars and sun.

But one does touch me most of all,
although it's plastic cheap.
The angel placed upon the top,
youth happiness to keep.

Christ's Birth

The beauty of Christmas is:
the Christmas tree ornament
fashioned by tiny hands
from glue and paper and glitter.

The carol of Christmas is:
the stillness of silence,
while pondering the true
reason we celebrate.

The joy of Christmas is:
the happiness felt deep
in the heart, while doing
something for someone else.

The peace of Christmas is:
the knowledge that,
even when alone, we are
a part of an infinite family.

Colors of Christmas

Gold, a gift the wise men chose
to give the newborn king.
It now reminds us give of self;
to others do we bring.

Silver – shining in the night
so high above his head.
This sweetest star now shines atop
the Christmas tree instead.

Green – renewal of the spring,
may we begin again.
His gift to us by birth and death –
awakens us from sin.

Red – the color of his blood,
he shed to make us free.
Born as Savior to mankind,
gave us eternity.

White – as snow that falls around
the day of Christ we see.
And I believe this color means
my Savior's purity.

Christmas Red

Red is the color of Santa Claus' suit,
that he wears on Christmas eve
delivering presents around the world –
to those who still believe.

Red is the color of candy cane stripe –
twisting 'round white on the staff.
Soft peppermint taste – sweet to the tongue,
in hopes it will last and last.

Red is the color of berries on vine
that stick out amidst the green.
A color of hope to animals cold,
as they feed through winter scene.

Red is the color of greatest of gifts.
Christ died, did not hesitate.
His loving blood shed as he gave up his life –
the real reason we celebrate.

Christmas Green

Color of the Christmas tree,
the evergreen behold.
Constantly renewing
begin again is told.

We think of green as being
new start of nature dear,
to see the rebirth everywhere
when looking far or near.

As Christmas time remembers
the coming of the King,
and as he gives his gift to us,
renews us, as the spring.

Candle

I light a candle to my Lord –
'twas born on Christmas day.
in a manger long ago,
the newborn Christ did lay.

And when the candles light the tree
we decorate to shame,
I see the light of Christ within
the candle's flickering flame.

A lighted candle on the seal
within the window bright,
a welcome home for someone lost,
just like my Savior's light.

Gifts

Wrapping donned with reindeer,
ribbon tied with a bow,
tassels hanging from the sack
and all that presents show.

To give one's self at Christmas,
to think of someone else,
the gifts we give to others
leaves nothing on the shelf.

But why this outward show of love?
This giving, we believe
is like unto the Magi,
to whom Christ did receive.

Their humble recognition
to whom they sought as King,
the show of adoration
the gifts had come to mean.

So, as we share our packages,
our mind to others, shifts.
However humble they might be,
our love is shown through gifts.

Christmas, Every Day

A bit of Christ-like living,
as well as celebrate.
The season comes December
each year, but not too late.

Along with decorations
and carols that we sing,
our hearts are filled with loving
and giving do we bring.

Thoughts turn to awing reverence,
our patience better now,
the greed replaced by sharing,
and peace within us show.

We recognize our Savior,
we enter in his way.
Just think what earth would be like –
with Christmas every day.

Christmas

Every year, we celebrate
the coming of the king.
Presents given represent
and carols do we sing.

We light the candles on the tree,
in windows, show the way.
And splendid parties we attend
before the Christmas day.

With decorations everywhere,
from wreath to flying deer.
The tree adorned with ornaments
and family drawing near.

This blessed month that leads up to
the holy day of light.
Above these things, remember
it is the "Mass of Christ".

Angels

Angels were there at the birth of the King.
Praise to the Savior, the angels did sing.
Just as He sent them to herald Christ's birth,
God will send angels to cheer those on earth.

Wreath

The wreath we hang upon our door
when Christmas time is here.
as welcome to our friends before
and all those we hold dear.

When think to more than circle is
unending in its curve.
I feel deep love respondent his,
replete – when him I serve.

For circle round upon his head
with horrid thorns complete,
that in his loving as they've said,
saves me at ransom seat.

So, in the sharing of my wreath
to all who come to give,
I'll show my God, that in his death,
his birth, has made me live.

What is Christmas For

Caroling in pick-up trucks,
a wreath upon the door,
warmly greeting neighbors,
what else is Christmas for?

A fire in the fireplace,
theme windows at the store,
festive wrap on packages,
what else is Christmas for?

Loved ones all around us;
how could we ask for more?
The warmth within December cold –
what else is Christmas for?

To humbly remember
the reason at its core –
our Savior born in Bethlehem,
what else is Christmas for?

Make-Believe Santa

Although I don't remember
that Santa Claus was real,
the presents set out Christmas morn,
the stockings had been filled.

Later, mama told me
truth was the family way –
that we were taught that Santa Claus
was make-believe, did say.

And of the Christmas visit –
it too, was make-believe.
Presents brought by mom and dad
is what we did receive.

When we went down to the store,
saw kids on Santa's knee.
The man inside that Santa suit
was helping make-believe.

Most choice of Santa's story –
his thought to do good things,
for Christ had taught to give of self –
the happiness it brings.

I do believe in Santa,
as make-believe, he's true.
And if we serve our fellow man,
Christ comes to visit too.

Christmas Memories

My own Chatty Cathy,
my stocking filled with stuff,
new clothing and new underwear
and all that other fluff.

Waking Christmas morning
by three or four o'clock,
sneaking to the living room
and daddy's chair that rocks.

Christmas morning breakfast
with family all around.
No special menu served here;
still, pleasant was the sound.

Watching family movies,
one, only one indoors.
Christmas morning mayhem
the year that I was born.

Opening the presents
still underneath the tree,
from one another given,
I couldn't wait to see.

Every year, my uncle
would Christmas, with us, share.
Mom would go and get him
from the home with nursing care.

My Christmas memories follow
through each and every year,
leave in my heart a yearning
to keep loved ones ever near.

Christmas Present

This is the Christmas present,
snow falling on the ground.
I'm sure that within hours
I'll hear the snowplow sound.

The neighborhood has put up lights,
my favorite has to be
way down the lane, the little house,
white icicles to see.

Out on each lawn, my neighbors put
their decorations guard.
Driveways marked with candy canes,
lights strung throughout the yard.

And some applaud the newest craze
while others need "Mylanta,"
I kinda like the air-filled deer
or motorcycle Santa.

The fiber optic Christmas trees
sure to attract the gaze,
with timely decorations like
the new transformers rage.

Activities like hayrides
updated from the past.
Now trailers pulled by Clydesdales
with hay bales - moving fast.

One thing that hasn't changed much,
I hope it never goes.
The small store at the dairy
with hot chocolate and fresh scones.

Still, one thing never changes,
why I look toward the season.
Remembering my Savior's birth,
the greatest of all reasons.

Carols

Sing we of the birth of the king,
raise our voices – to him we sing
in remembrance of his birth,
Christ the Savior of the earth.

With the joyous music raise,
all our humble faithful praise.
When to those who love him well,
let your voices ever swell.

In the singing of our song,
praises to our Lord belong.
Carols that we sing this day
are to our God, as though we pray.

So, Christmas carols we shall voice,
and in our Savior, Christ rejoice.
To share this time with those we love,
while giving thanks to God above.

Carols in July

Songs unto my Savior,
the carols that we sing
at Christmas to remember –
and thoughts of Christ to bring.

Once Christmas season's over,
on Him we still rely.
To continue Christmas spirit,
I sing carols in July.

Old Fashioned Christmas

Take me back to an old-fashioned Christmas,
a Christmas with family ties,
and maybe a sleigh drawn by horses
as pictured by Currier and Ives.

With old fashioned candies and décor,
quite simple, what happiness brings.
The truth behind old fashioned Christmas –
is everything family means.

Christmas Lights

In darkness, I see a candle's light
shining bright in a window at home.
It's a welcome to every threadbare heart
and for me, it's relief to come.

In darkness, I see the light of a star
shining over a Bethlehem barn.
It announces the birth of the newborn king
who will save the soul so forlorn.

In darkness, I see the light of my God
shining through my shadow of sin.
We celebrate Christmas, remember His gift,
Christ, the Lord, the Savior of men.

Holly

Holly and ivy and mistletoe too,
sleigh bells on horses, and ice skates for shoes,
warm woolen mittens to match scarf and hat,
carolers singing, not a little bit flat.

Old fashioned candies – been all made by hand
from old family recipes, best in the land.
Wassail and eggnog and chocolate delight
parties and dinners before Christmas night.

Everyone going from here – to and fro,
busily finishing, ready to go.
For last minute shopping and trimming the tree,
wrapping the presents, to open with glee.

At last, is the moment we all go to bed,
each knowing that Santa's about in his sled.
All Christmas season, the shopping , the play
has led to this moment, has come to this day.

Still something is stirring – way deep down inside.
a yearning, a feeling, a strong moving tide.
But, what is forgotten, please memory bring
the reason we celebrate, Christ born to be king.

Gold, Frankincense and Myrrh

The gifts the Wisemen brought him,
gold, frankincense and myrrh.
Each had a special meaning,
most people would concur.

Gold, a most impressive ore –
then, was a sign of wealth,
mostly used as barter,
important more than health.

Frankincense, an incense,
sweet smelling resin gum,
light yellow / brown in color,
opaque in purest form.

Myrrh is too, a resin gum,
reddish brown in hue.
Used in working with the dead,
in perfume, incense too.

When presented to the Lord,
they were as precious gems.
No matter meaning of the gifts –
they were to honor Him.

Herald

I heard the bells on Christmas day,
angelic choirs did sing.
Peace on earth, good will to men –
this holy infant did bring.

But wait – while the bells of Heaven rang.
love shown by the new star's light –
for when the bells did herald His birth,
I was in the choir that night.

This Night

Behold this night, a bright new star
shines down upon a town.
And stabled there, a newborn child,
the Lord of all renown.

Behold this night, a manger warm –
complete with fresh new grass,
And laying there – a King of Kings,
prophesy come to pass.

Behold this night – in nearby fields
the shepherds watch their sheep.
And came to them, an angel,
God's promises to keep.

Behold this night, the angels sing.
In multitude, they say:
"Peace on the earth, good will to men
upon this holy day."

Behold this night, this Holy night –
man's Savior, He is born.
No greater gift was ever g'vn
than on this Holy morn.

Holy Night

What peace must follow quiet streets,
a new star shines above.
O, holy night, when come to earth
such proof of Father's love.

For God above knows mercy,
a Savior come to men.
This tiny newborn child
to save the world from sin.

For now, is celebration
and choirs of Heaven sing –
Good will to men and peace on earth –
this holy night doeth bring.

The Star

A star is shining up above
the miracle on earth –
a new and brightly shining star
accompanies this birth.

How oft do heavenly bodies
resound the forecast true.
This brightest star shines over
the king so fresh and new.

Shining down a pillar,
a shaft of light so pure,
and pointing to the cradle,
a manger holding sure.

This star, a holy wonder,
a sign from up above,
to tell the world this child,
God's son, is of God's love.

Do You Know?

There He lay, the newborn Savior;
so new to this world of sin.
Did He know, as He gazed in His mother's eyes;
did He know what his mission was then?

When she watched her new son sleeping;
just sent from heaven above.
Did she know He would give His life for her?
Did she know it would be out of love?

As the shepherds knelt before Him;
being led by the angel's light.
Did they know, as they saw His innocent face;
did they know who He was that night?

Christmas season is spent reflecting,
for He is the chosen one.
Do you know who it was that was born that night?
Do you know it was God's own son?

Mary

A girl, behold – a virgin,
so fair and virtuous, she.
Chosen to be the mother of Christ,
to raise Him at her knee.

She must have had unfailing faith
and trust in God above.
To have an angel tell her –
she'd bear the one – God's love.

How must she'd been believing –
to tell her chosen spouse
though true to him, expecting
God's son, to raise in course.

And on that special Christmas night,
brought forth her first born son.
She held Him close within her arms –
Mary, a chosen one.

Joseph

What kind of man must Joseph been,
how faithful to the Lord.
How kind, how loving when he heard
that Mary knew God's word.

To know his first born was not his,
his wife to have God's son –
that he would raise Christ as his own
and still his love was one.

To see the babe in Mary's arms,
to sense the mortal's wish,
and father Him until He knew
the mission that was His.

To teach, to love this oldest son
to mentor Him with love
until the day that Joseph left
this earth to go above.

Stable

How lowly and how humble,
am I in human thought.
A simple stone built structure,
only by animals sought.

And yet, one night, came glory
for this humblest abode.
Chosen above the others
as a shelter for my Lord.

Before this night were many births
I've covered, warmth to give –
but on this night, this newborn,
a God had come to live.

In my being, prophesy
fulfilled, the King adorn.
Stronger still – my experience –
I watched my God be born.

Peace on Earth

Tonight an angel came to earth
to herald the birth of the Christ.
And joining him, a multitude –
glory God who would pay our price.

"Fear not" the shepherds heard him say –
"...Behold... tidings of great joy...
for unto you is born this day...
a Savior..." (a baby boy).

"And this shall be a sign... to you...
the babe wrapped in swaddling clothes,
lying in a manger."
"Christ the Lord." He did propose.

And suddenly a multitude
of heavenly host appeared,
praising God and saying
in a manner to be heard.

"Glory to God in the highest
and on earth, (should there be) peace,
good will toward (the) men (of earth)."
all eternal pain to cease.

And now, two thousand years abide,
remember the birth of our King.
Say "Glory to God in the highest" –
on earth, peace we hope to bring.

Luke 2:10-14

Shepherd

This cloudless night, in stillness,
the silent stars do shine.
We sit, intently watching
the flock, these sheep of mine.

But lo, I see a stranger
appears above mine eyes.
What glory shines around us,
what fear to my demise.

"Fear not...." The angel tells us –
"Good tidings" for to bring,
in Bethlehem, a Savior
is born to be the king.

"For lying in a manger,
wrapped snug in swaddling clothes,
ye shall find the son of God,
Christ – Lord ye do suppose."

My fear has turned to wondering,
a multitude join force.
They praise the everlasting God
and offer peace to earth.

The angels gone before us,
let's go to Bethlehem.
We find the babe as told us,
a lamb among the lambs.

I can't contain my feelings,
must share with all I know.
I saw the Christ, who was foretold,
and angels – it is so.

Luke 2:8-20

The Shepherds

It's right, the first to see him
were shepherds from the field.
The men who watched out over
the lambs, the newborn yield.

For in the darkness of the night
the angels did appear,
to herald Jesus' foretold birth,
to all whose hearts would hear.

These men, protectors through the dark—
to save from evil's toll,
the first to see the Savior
who saves the threatened soul.

Humble Beginnings

A barn, a hay rack for a bed,
no hospital or nurse.
With straw for bedding, laid to sleep,
no warmth, no comfort purse.

All privacy included –
the animals around.
Patient, ever watching
there on the birthing grounds.

Long strips of cloth called swaddling,
first clothing ever worn,
with humble mother close beside –
a smile to adorn.

The humblest beginning
shows not how great his worth –
for lowly was the first day of
the Savior of the earth.

The Magi

The star they saw and followed,
a newborn king they sought
to worship and to offer
the presents that they brought.

These men who came a distance –
from where their east home lies.
For who else saw the prophecy –
It's true, these men were wise.

Bethlehem

I watched you sleep, just hours old
within my stable small.
I know you are the son of God –
to save men from the fall.

I see the shepherds come to see,
the angels sing your birth.
I know that star shines high above –
the greatest gift to earth.

I see the wise men follow
that star so new and bright.
They come to see the Savior
with gifts they bring tonight.

I feel I hold you in my arms
today you are the lamb –
to grow, become the Savior.
Born in me – I am Bethlehem.

Donkey

Upon my back, I carried
the mother, yet to be.
Her travel be less anxious
than walking would to see.

The night that she delivered,
I saw the newborn Christ.
He was to be Redeemer,
to give the people life.

When Harod sent the soldiers
and Joseph saw the dream,
I carried Mary and the babe
to safety from hate's stream.

I only am a donkey –
yet humble gifts, no lack.
For, the greatest king of all –
I carried on my back.

Livestock

They shared their home for birth of God,
    they gave the warmth of hay,
they loaned their manger – where they fed
    in which the Christ child lay.

They witnessed Mary bring him forth,
    the babe, the king, her son.
Who, also, was the son of God –
    God's only begotten one.

They watched him sleep quite warm within
    the hay so fresh and new.
This first day of his journey long,
    a kingdom to ensue.

They knew his reign would not be one
    of terror or of hate,
but one of love and patience rare,
    teach, enter in the gate.

So in their midst, it seems quite fair,
    the new king would be found,
and, when men came to see the Christ,
    that animals were 'round.

Manger

Made of wood, though second rate,
used planks with holes and knots.
For animals, the feed to put –
the purpose of the box.

Yet, one night, one holy night
the box was filled with hay.
A first time mother given birth
and there, her son did lay.

At Christmas we remember,
humble hearts we do achieve.
To ponder this – our Savior,
a manger did first receive.

Mary's Lullaby

Rock-a-bye, rock- a-bye, little baby of mine.
I'll rock you, my sweetheart 'til morning sun shines.
For morrow is coming, the whole world to see,
but just for this moment, belong just to me.

Tonight heaven's angels herald your birth –
that you are God's son, the only on earth.
And under the star light of sky's newest show,
wrapped snuggly you lay in a manger so low.

For now, I shall hold you, embracing you tight,
I'll save you, my child from evil tonight.
Wanting to keep you to me – all alone,
knowing, my love, you belong to the throne.

My Son

My first born child, how precious are you,
perfect innocence, I see.
I'll hold you – be safe – within my arms,
to shelter you while at my knee.

I know that you father is no man of earth.
He's the God of the heaven above.
Your name shall be Jesus, for all men, you'll die.
but, for now, I'll defend you, my love.

I see in your gaze, just a few minutes old.
Have you knowledge of anything yet?
When will you know of your mission in life –
until then, shall I keep your needs met.

As you close your sweet eyes, surrounded by love,
I'll watch over you as you shall sleep.
And as you shall grow, dear son of mine,
I'll protect as a shepherd would sheep.

What is this? Am I seeing a gleam in your eye?
You're aware of my lullaby sung.
You're saying to me, you remember above,
you know you are God's own son.

Christ, Jesus

For unto you is born this day –
the herald angel did sing,
and mountains shouted back to say –
be peace on earth to bring.

Go to Bethlehem and see
the Christ child has been born.
What wonder, miracle to be,
this early Christmas morn.

Within a manger, you shall find
him wrapped in swaddling clothes.
The future Savior, he shall bind…
The air around him glows.

This tiny baby, such a lamb –
the heavens give him laud.
Yes, born this night in Bethlehem –
Christ, Jesus, son of God.

Prophesy

Babe laying in a manger
within a stable small.
Laying there, in swaddling clothes,
the Savior of us all.

He would grow and learn men's ways,
would teach the greater law,
would heal the sick and feed the crowd.
Fame spread from what they saw.

He thwarted evil doings,
was vocal 'bout the bad.
They tried to trap Him in His words,
which doings made Him sad.

Arrested and mistreated,
He died for all mankind,
To come again as King of Kings,
eternity to bind.

There laying in that manger,
Christ, Jesus, God's own son,
to save the world from all its sin –
was prophesied to come.

King of Kings

How sweetly lays the King of Kings,
within a manger, sleep.
This holy night, a savior born –
God's promises to keep.

His coming shared with all who'd hear,
a virgin to give birth
in Bethlehem, Immanuel,
Christ, Jesus come to earth.

Around His cradle, come to see,
sent by the angels' song,
abiding shepherds in the field
who heard the heavenly throng.

This humble night, it's peaceful realm,
amidst the war torn land,
a newborn babe, who'll save my soul,
the prophesies to stand.

Oh King of Kings – how great thou art,
my heart loves longer still.
For Thou wert born that holy night,
the Father's plan to seal.

My Savior's Birth

Though He was born in spring time,
in December we celebrate.
It's not the date that matters,
but why, that makes me quake.

A child was born – an infant –
as helpless as we all.
To grow, become the Savior
for every human soul.

But on this night, a stable,
the first home He would know.
A small, yet comfort, dwelling
with livestock guarding so.

A star, foretold, to shine upon
the birth of God's own son.
To come, but once, unto the world –
redemption to be done.

Wise Men

I saw the new star in the sky,
the night that it appeared.
From here in Persia, shining bright
over Israel, it "teared"

In awe, I called my dearest friends
to come and go with me –
the wonderment this star has brought,
the mystery to see.

Yes, up above fulfilling grace
of prophesy foretold –
a king is born beneath this star,
a king I must behold.

How long had mankind waited for
this thing to come to pass –
said by the prophets long ago
whose coming's here at last.

We got our things together,
prepared the journey long.
We're setting off to find the King
and bring him gifts of home.

Our journey long and arduous,
the caravan moves well –
Jerusalem, the capital
of where the Jews do dwell.

Entering the city walls,
asked of the newborn king.
"We've seen his star far in the east,
are come to worship him."

King Harod called to see us,
inquired of the star.
How long ago did it appear,
that we would come so far.

And when we gave him answer,
to Bethlehem we're sent.
"Search for the child diligent,
I too, can worship, spent."

Leaving Harod's presence,
the star before us goes
to shine above the child young –
the joy within us grows.

We saw the child, finally,
there with his mother sweet.
Down to our knees, we dropped with love,
to worship at his feet.

Presented we, our gifts to him,
the king we long had sought.
We offered gold, we offered myrrh,
and frankincense we'd brought.

(next page)

Time had come for us to go,
with heavy hearts we turned
to leave the king we came to see,
for all our lives we yearned.

That night, I slept, I saw a dream,
God warned of Harod's fray.
When to depart, to go back home,
must go a different way.

So, we departed, praising
the everlasting God,
heading east another way
unto our homeland sod.

Throughout my life I'd longed for
the prophesy fulfilled,
to live to see my Savior,
to worship and be "healed".

For all the people of the earth,
all prophesy that's been.
How few had known the star was for –
the Christ. We were wise men.

Matt 2: 1-13

The Christmas Visit

On the twenty fourth day of December,
as midnight was drawing nigh;
my Christmas rush was over,
I gave a well earned sigh.

Carefully wrapped were the presents,
now sitting beneath the tree.
Each with a bow and a ribbon,
looking most fashionably.

The tree itself – stood there glowing,
never mattered if fake or if real.
With specially chosen ornaments
to give it such great appeal.

On the fireplace mantle were stockings,
each hung there with loving care,
and waiting for Santa's visit,
to be filled by him with flair.

All of the decorations
we had placed throughout the house
were cheery and ever festive –
down to the little Yule mouse.

Now, it was very quiet,
the children asleep in their beds.
Each dreaming of Christmas morning
with visions of toys in their heads.

I said "good night" to my sweetheart
who, moments ago, left the room.
My eyelids were growing heavy,
I'd be going to bed very soon.

I sat and I gazed at the Christmas tree,
thinking of gifts I'd receive.
I must have briefly nodded off,
Eyes opened to what I believed.

Santa was there, by the stockings,
having come down the chimney black.
Out of his bag, he brought presents
to each stocking, he filled with no lack.

He turned around and he saw me,
eyes twinkling as he stood there.
So peaceful, I felt in his presence;
I knew I had nary a care.

I glanced around at the trimmings,
each perfectly set in its place.
Then, suddenly, everything vanished
and again, I looked at his face.

His eyes glowed with love everlasting;
his whiskers, no longer were gray.
The Santa I knew as a child,
I saw was changing away.

(next page)

His boots, I saw become sandals;
his coat, a robe, crimson red.
His garments became a tan tunic;
his hat, a thorn ring round his head.

He looked quite a bit thinner,
though, still a little robust.
Around him, a aura of giving
as someone I knew I could trust.

And then, to me, understanding
came flooding from heaven above.
The reason we celebrate Christmas,
are two gifts that were given with love.

The first – the newborn Savior,
who was sent to redeem those on earth
by a loving Heavenly Father.
His gift given us at Christ's birth.

And then, the greatest gift of all –
no presents we give, can compare.
Our loving Savior died for us;
the pains of my sins, He would bear.

The clock on the mantle chimed midnight.
I awoke to find all as it was.
I smiled a smile of awareness,
and got up from my chair, then I paused.

As Christians, we believe we give presents,
for the wise men gave gifts to the king.
Not of gold or myrrh or frankincense,
but more modern and chic do we bring.

Then, I heard the soft jingling of sleigh bells,
and heard Santa exclaim "He is real."
Christ, the Savior, was born – or – so long ago,
but His spirit remains with us still.

About the Author

Joyce E. Larsen is a native of Bountiful, Utah, one of nine children. She was educated at the University of Utah.

She is the author of four books – two poetry and two children's books (based on characters created by her mother), and is working on a third book of poetry.

A spiritualist at heart, she leans toward religious and inspirational topics as can be witnessed in her writings.

Joyce is a down to earth personality who lives on a small two acre piece of horse property she calls "What Joy Farm" in Erda, Utah.

Made in the USA
Middletown, DE
02 March 2022

61983563R00120